THE BEST
CATS
EVER

MAINE COONS ARE THE BEST!

Elaine Landau

LERNER PUBLICATIONS COMPANY · MINNEAPOLIS

Lerner Publications Company
A division of Lerner Publishing Group, Inc.
241 First Avenue North
Minneapolis, MN 55401 U.S.A.

Website address: www.lernerbooks.com

Library of Congress Cataloging-in-Publication Data

Landau, Elaine.
    Maine coons are the best! / by Elaine Landau.
      p.   cm. — (The best cats ever)
    Includes index.
    ISBN 978-0-7613-6426-9 (lib. bdg. : alk. paper)
    1. Maine coon cat. I. Title.
  SF449.M34L36 2011
  636.8'3—dc22   2010008080

Manufactured in the United States of America
1 - CG - 12/31/10

TABLE OF CONTENTS

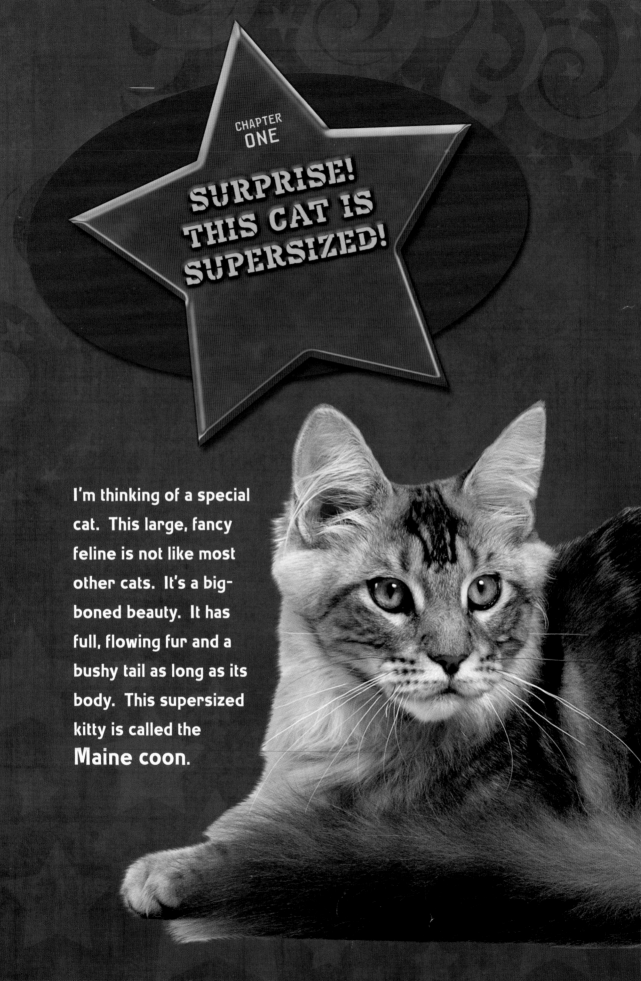

SURPRISE! THIS CAT IS SUPERSIZED!

I'm thinking of a special cat. This large, fancy feline is not like most other cats. It's a big-boned beauty. It has full, flowing fur and a bushy tail as long as its body. This supersized kitty is called the **Maine coon.**

A Big Hunk of Cat

The Maine coon is a heavy cat.

The average house cat weighs from 6 to 15 pounds (3 to 7 kilograms). But there's nothing average about a Maine coon. A large male can weigh as much as 20 pounds (9 kg). Females are usually smaller than males. Female Maine coons can weigh as much as 15 pounds (7 kg). Most of these big kitties have 2 to 3 inches (5 to 8 centimeters) of thick, shaggy fur. That's a lot of cat to love!

THE NAME GAME

Maine coons are great cats. And every great cat needs a great name. Do any of these fit your playful kitty?

STORMY

Bigfoot

Venus

Rocky

Hercules

Bruiser

Tiny

Shaggy

Dusty

Zeus

Ready for Winter

Maine coons are built for cold weather. Their giant paws look like snowshoes. They have tufts of fur on top of their large ears. And water slips right off their fluffy coats. On extra-cold days, a Maine coon can even wrap up in its long, bushy tail for warmth.

A Maine coon's paws make walking on snow a snap.

A Cat of Many Colors

Maine coons come in all sorts of colors, such as solid white, black, or gray. Maine coons come in different patterns as well. The striped brown Maine coon is the most common. It makes up more than half of all Maine coons.

These cats are all Maine coons even though they are different colors.

The Sweetest Sound

Think all cats sound alike? Then you haven't heard the Maine coon. These cats enjoy talking to their owners. Maine coons have their own special sound. It's sort of like a purr, a chirp, and a meow all at once. Though the Maine coon is a large cat, its voice is soft and lovely.

More Than a Pretty Face

Most Maine coons are fun companions. These charming cats can quickly steal your heart. They'll follow you from room to room. They love to play and want you to play with them. Maine coons are even good with dogs and small children. Their owners think they have the best cats ever!

Is That a Cat Or a Lion?

In 2006, a Maine coon from Chicago, Illinois, made history. The Maine coon, named Leo, set the Guinness World Record for longest cat. Leo measured 48 inches (122 cm) from nose to tail. That's almost twice as long as the average house cat!

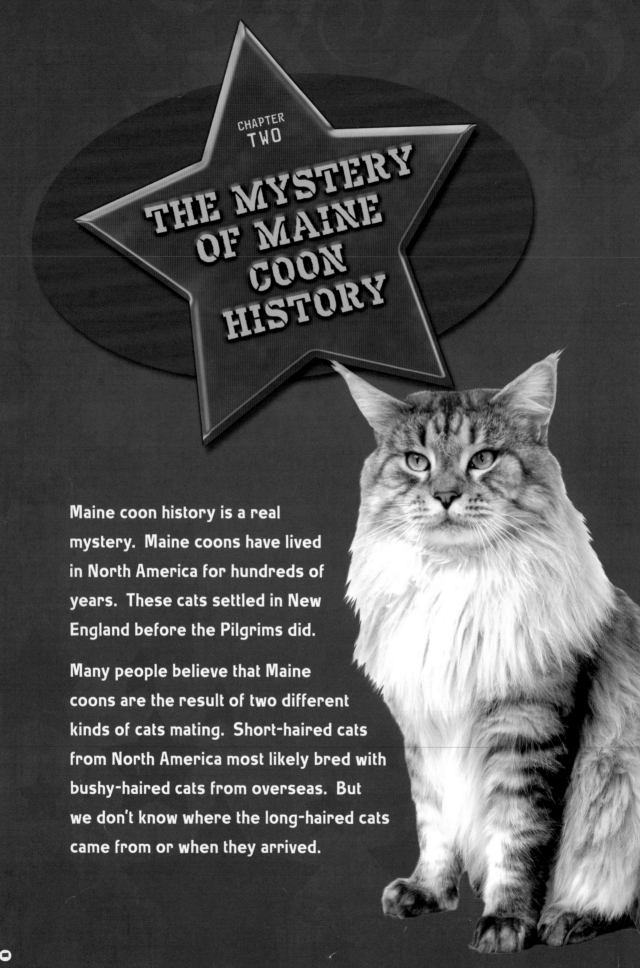

CHAPTER TWO

THE MYSTERY OF MAINE COON HISTORY

Maine coon history is a real mystery. Maine coons have lived in North America for hundreds of years. These cats settled in New England before the Pilgrims did.

Many people believe that Maine coons are the result of two different kinds of cats mating. Short-haired cats from North America most likely bred with bushy-haired cats from overseas. But we don't know where the long-haired cats came from or when they arrived.

A Viking Cat?

Vikings traveled from Europe to other lands, such as North America.

Explorers called Vikings from northern Europe sailed to North America more than one thousand years ago. The Vikings kept cats on board their ships. These frisky kitties helped with rat control.

When the sailors went ashore, the cats often followed them. Long-haired Viking cats may have bred with local cats to create the Maine coon. Maine coons look similar to cats that once traveled with the Vikings.

Captain Charles Coon's Cats

Maine coon fans have more than one hunch about when the cat first appeared in North America. The coast of the state of Maine had many busy seaports in the 1800s. Traders and sailors from Europe stopped there often. One legend says that a British soldier named Captain Charles Coon brought long-haired cats onshore with him when he was in the area. Maybe these cats are the Maine coon's real relatives.

Captain Charles Coon might have taken cats onto this shore in Maine more than two hundred years ago.

A MAINE COON MIX-UP

Some Maine coons look like a cross between a raccoon (left) and a cat. They have fluffy ringed tails and dark gray fur. Modern scientists know that the Maine coon isn't really related to the raccoon. But the Maine coon's raccoonlike appearance might be how the cat got its name.

A Hardy Kitty

Not just any cat could have survived New England's harsh winters. No matter where Maine coons came from, they needed a thick, shaggy coat for warmth. They also had to be strong and sturdy to hunt small prey. Wild Maine coons were able to take down large rabbits and groundhogs.

The Main Cat in Maine

People in Maine grew quite fond of the Maine coon. Their pride in the kitty really swelled in 1895. That year, New York City hosted the country's first National Cat Show.

The National Cat Show featured all sorts of beautiful cats. Slim, sleek Siamese cats were there. Pretty Persians were present too. But a Maine coon named Cosey won the show's top prize.

A man waits for his Maine coon to be judged at a cat show in New York.

A STATELY STATE CAT

All the fifty states have state symbols. Maine's state tree is the eastern white pine. Its state insect is the honeybee. Can you guess what the state cat is? It's the Maine coon!

Cosey became a Maine coon superstar. Soon lots of people wanted a Maine coon. These days, Maine coons are the second most popular cat breed in the United States.

THE RIGHT CAT FOR YOU?

You've fallen in love with the Maine coon. You've got to have one. You think it's time to pick out a Maine coon of your very own.

But wait! Is the Maine coon really right for you? Let's take a closer look.

Is Bigger Always Better?

Maine coons are sweet, but they aren't petite. Your Maine coon will have a big appetite. It will be your job to make sure it gets enough to eat each day.

Heavy cats are also hard to carry. Your Maine coon will be traveling in a cat carrier. This carrier adds more weight to the load. Will you be able to easily take your cat to where it needs to go?

A Main coon is a large, hungry cat. Don't forget to feed it healthy food!

Gotta Groom 'Em

People will admire your Maine coon's long, shaggy coat—but only if you take the time to care for it. Maine coons shed (lose) their old hair. You'll need to comb through your cat's fur twice a week to remove loose hairs. Are you up for it?

This girl takes time to brush her Maine coon.

BOY OR GIRL?

There are certain differences between male and female Maine coons. Males are said to be more playful and frisky. They tend to pick out a favorite human as their best buddy. Females are a bit quieter. They usually get close to the whole family.

Do You Want a Cat That's Like a Dog?

Maine coons are very active cats. They can be tons of fun. Some people even say Maine coons behave like dogs. Your Maine coon will want to be by your side. It might even want to play when you're trying to do homework. Make sure you have time for a cat that needs a playmate.

Be prepared to give your Maine coon lots of attention. Do you spend most of your time out of the house with friends? Do you have loads of after-school activities? If so, a bird or a fish might be a better choice.

A Costly Kitty

Maine coons can be costly. They are purebred cats. Breeders charge a lot of money for their kittens. Prices for a Maine coon kitten can range from about six hundred to two thousand dollars. Can your family afford a high-priced pet? Be sure to discuss this with them.

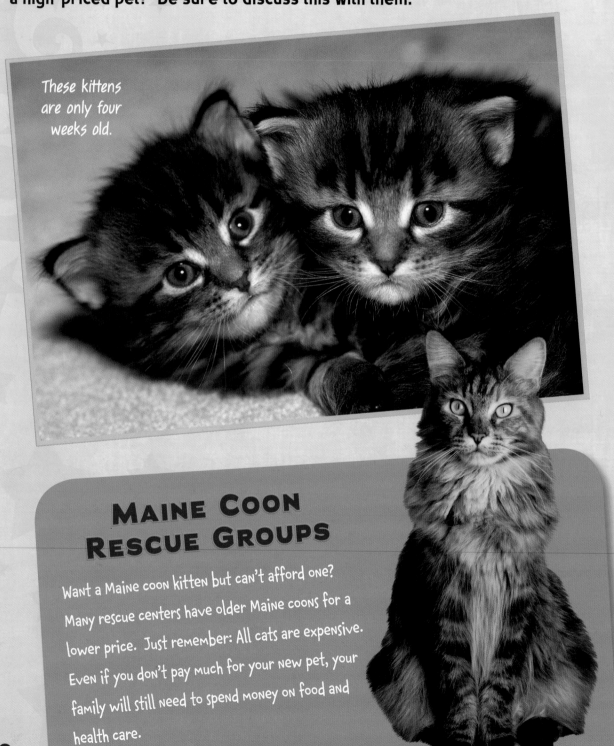

These kittens are only four weeks old.

MAINE COON RESCUE GROUPS

Want a Maine coon kitten but can't afford one? Many rescue centers have older Maine coons for a lower price. Just remember: All cats are expensive. Even if you don't pay much for your new pet, your family will still need to spend money on food and health care.

A Maine coon is not for everyone. Have you decided if it's right for you? If it is, you're in luck. A big, furry friend is about to join your family. Enjoy every minute of it!

CHAPTER FOUR

WELCOME YOUR MAINE COON

What an exciting day! You're bringing home your Maine coon.

Stock Up

Make this a great day for your Maine coon too. Be sure you have everything you need for your new cat. Buy it some basic supplies. Here's a starter list of things you'll need:

- food and water bowls

- cat food

- litter box

- kitty litter

- brush and wide-tooth steel comb

- scratching post

- cat carrier

WATER, WATER EVERYWHERE

Maine coons love water. Many play with the water in their water bowl. They delight in a drippy faucet. Some will even nap in an empty bathtub!

Visit the Vet

Take your Maine coon to a veterinarian soon.

That's a doctor who takes care of animals.

They are called vets for short.

The vet will check your Maine coon's health. Your kitty will also get the shots it needs to stay healthy. Take your cat back to the vet for regular checkups. And take your Maine coon straight to the vet if it gets sick.

A veterinarian should regularly check your Maine coon's health.

Feeding Fluffy

Give your cat a healthful diet that keeps it
frisky and fit. Ask your vet what to feed your
Maine coon. Don't give your cat
table scraps. This can lead to
unhealthful weight gain.

PLAY BALL!

Maine coons love playing with balls. Some of these cats even like to play fetch. Try tossing a cat toy to your Maine coon. You'll have a ball together!

Watch Out for Molting Season

Maine coons shed their fur once or twice a year. This is known as molting. During these times, you'll have to groom your cat more often. It's a lot of work. But it will keep your cat's coat healthy and clean.

You and Your Maine Coon

You and your Maine coon will be BFF (best friends forever). But that means more than just playing together. To really be a best friend, you'll need to take good care of your Maine coon.

Your Maine coon might want to cuddle up with you while you read.

Remember that your cat is a living thing. It needs love and attention even when you're busy or tired. Be the kind of owner your Maine coon can be proud of. You'll be proud of yourself too!

GLOSSARY

breed: a particular type of cat. Cats of the same breed have the same body shape and general features. *Breed* can also refer to producing kittens.

breeder: someone who mates cats to produce a particular kind of cat

coat: a cat's fur

diet: the food your cat eats

frisky: very lively or playful

groom: to clean, brush, and trim a cat's coat

molting: the process through which an animal's outer covering of fur comes off so that a new covering can grow

purebred: a cat whose parents are of the same breed

rescue center: a shelter where stray and abandoned cats are kept until they are adopted

shed: to lose fur

veterinarian: a doctor who treats animals. Veterinarians are called vets for short.

FOR MORE INFORMATION

Books

Brecke, Nicole, and Patricia M. Stockland. *Cats You Can Draw*. Minneapolis: Millbrook Press, 2010. Perfect for cat lovers, this colorful book teaches readers how to draw many popular cat breeds.

Brown, Ruth. *Gracie the Lighthouse Cat*. London: Andersen Press, 2011. Gracie the lighthouse cat and Grace Darling, the lighthouse keeper's daughter, both have an adventure one very windy night.

Harris, Trudy. *Tally Cat Keeps Track*. Minneapolis: Millbrook Press, 2011. Tally McNally is a cat who loves to tally—but one day, he gets into a jam. Will his friends find a way to help him?

Landau, Elaine. *Your Pet Cat*. Rev. ed. New York: Children's Press, 2007. This title is a good guide for young people on choosing and caring for a cat.

Scheunemann, Pam. *Marvelous Maine Coons*. Edina, MN: ABDO, 2010. This book provides information on buying and living with a Maine coon cat.

Websites

ASPCA Kids

http://www.aspca.org/aspcakids
Check out this website for helpful hints on caring for a cat and other pets.

For Kids: About Cats

http://kids.cfa.org
Be sure to visit this website for kids on cats and cat shows. Don't miss the link to some fun games as well.

Maine Coon Rescue

http://www.mainecoonrescue.net
This nationwide nonprofit group helps Maine coons find loving homes.

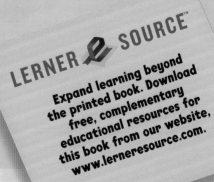

LERNER e SOURCE™

Expand learning beyond the printed book. Download free, complementary educational resources for this book from our website, www.lerneresource.com.

Index

Photo Acknowledgments

The images in this book are used with the permission of: backgrounds © iStockphoto.com/javarman3 and © iStockphoto.com/Julie Fisher; © iStockphoto.com/Michael Balderas, p. 1; © Ekaterina Cherkashina/Dreamstime.com, pp. 4-5; © Fiona Green, pp. 5, 17, 18 (top), 21 (top); © NaturePL/SuperStock, pp. 6 (main), 13; © GK Hart/Vikki Hart/The Image Bank/Getty Images, p. 6 (inset); © Juniors Bildarchiv/Alamy, pp. 7 (top), 15, 18 (bottom), 27 (bottom), 28-29; © Kirill Vorobyev/Dreamstime.com, p. 7 (bottom); © iStockphoto.com/Karen Town , p. 8; © David Coleman/Dreamstime.com, p. 9; © Elena Butinova/Dreamstime.com, pp. 10-11; © Ive Close Images/Alamy, p. 11; © John J. Henderson/Dreamstime.com, p. 12 (left); © Tom Price/Dreamstime.com, p. 12 (right); © JEFF CHRISTENSEN/Reuters/CORBIS, p. 14 (top); © Eric Isselée/Dreamstime.com, pp. 14 (bottom), 21 (bottom), 25 (left); © Doris Heinrichs-Fotolia.com, p. 16; © Ulrike Schanz/Animals Animals, pp. 16-17; © Brigitte Sire/Workbook Stock/Getty Images, p. 19; © IndexStock/SuperStock, p. 20 (top); © Tommy Flynn/Photonica/Getty Images, p. 20 (bottom); © Linncurrie/Dreamstime.com, p. 22; © Agita Leimane/Dreamstime.com, p. 23 (top); © Eti Swinford/Dreamstime.com, p. 23 (2nd from top); © Mike Bond/Dreamstime.com, p. 23 (3rd from top); © Mark Taylor/NPL//Minden Pictures, p. 23 (bottom); © GK Hart/Vikki Hart/Taxi/Getty Images, p. 24; © Jose Manuel Gelpi Diaz/Dreamstime.com, p. 25 (right); © Joyce Michaud/Dreamstime.com, pp. 26, 29.

Front cover: © Elena Butinova/Dreamstime.com.
Back cover: © Eric Isselée/Dreamstime.com.